Children's Authors

Dr. Seuss

Mae Woods

ABDO Publishing Company

visit us at
www.abdopub.com

Published by ABDO Publishing Company, 4940 Viking Drive, Suite 622, Edina, Minnesota 55435. Copyright © 2000 Abdo Consulting Group, Inc., Pentagon Tower, P.O. Box 36036, Minneapolis, Minnesota 55435 USA. International copyrights reserved in all countries. No part of this book may be reproduced in any form without written permission from the publisher.

Printed in the United States.

Photos: Corbis, AP/Wideworld
Editors: Bob Italia, Tamara L. Britton, Kate A. Furlong
Art Direction: Pat Laurel

Library of Congress Cataloging-in-Publication Data

Woods, Mae.
    Dr. Seuss / Mae Woods.
        p. cm. -- (Children's authors)
    Includes bibliographical references and index.
    ISBN 1-57765-110-3
        1. Seuss, Dr.--Juvenile literature. 2. Authors, American--20th
    century--Biography--Juvenile literature. 3. Illustrators--United
    States--Biography--Juvenile literature. 4. Children's literature --Authorship--Juvenile
    literature. [1. Seuss, Dr. 2. Authors, American. 3. Illustrators.] I. Title.

PS3513.E2 Z974 2000
813'.52--dc21
[B]   00-038585

Contents

How Dr. Seuss
Got His Name

Dr. Seuss was the **pen name** of Theodor Seuss Geisel. His friends called him Ted. When Ted was in college, he **edited** the school humor magazine. One day, Ted had a party late at night. When the party got too loud, Ted's **landlord** called the **dean**. Ted got in trouble, and he couldn't edit the magazine anymore. But Ted did not stop drawing cartoons. He signed them with his middle name to fool the dean.

After college, Ted continued to sign his work "Seuss." When he got his first job, he added the title "Dr." Later, he picked Theophrastus as a first name and his pen name was complete. That's how Dr. Theophrastus Seuss came to life. Dr. Seuss soon became one of America's favorite storytellers.

Dr. Seuss in his studio

Early Life

*T*ed Geisel was born on March 2, 1904, in Springfield, Massachusetts. His father was Theodor Robert Geisel, and his mother was Henrietta Seuss. Both his parents' families came from Germany and lived near Ted. Ted and his older sister Marnie grew up speaking German as well as English.

The Geisels' home was a few blocks away from Forest Park Zoo. Ted's father was a park official there. He often took young Ted to the zoo. When Ted came home, he drew pictures of the animals. The creatures Ted drew never looked like the real animals. They had long, long ears or odd feet. His mother loved his drawings and always encouraged Ted to use his imagination.

Ted took his first art class in high school. The teacher did not let Ted draw like he wanted to. She wanted him to follow too many rules. He dropped out of her class and managed the soccer team instead. Ted never took another art class.

Dr. Seuss learned to draw by creating pictures of zoo animals like these zebras from the San Diego Zoo.

First Jobs

*A*t age 17, Ted left home to go to Dartmouth College in New Hampshire. He planned to become an English teacher. He **edited** and wrote for the *Jack-O-Lantern*, Dartmouth's humor magazine. When he graduated, he went to England to study at Lincoln College at Oxford University. There, he became friends with another American student, Helen Palmer.

Helen thought Ted was clever and she loved his animal drawings. Helen encouraged Ted to **concentrate** on drawing instead of studying to become a teacher. Ted realized he did not really want to be a teacher. He wanted to be a writer and an illustrator.

When Ted returned from England, he tried to sell his illustrations. But nobody would buy them. Finally, he sold a cartoon to the *Saturday Evening Post*. He moved to New York City and soon found a job drawing comics at *Judge* magazine. Ted and Helen got married on November 29, 1927.

One of Ted's cartoons in *Judge* magazine joked about an insect spray called Flit. Instead of being angry about the joke, the H.K. McCann Advertising Agency, the makers of Flit ads, offered him a job. For the next 17 years, Ted wrote advertisements. He was finally a well-known, successful illustrator.

Lincoln College at Oxford University

Dr. Seuss in the Army

*O*n December 7, 1941, Japanese planes bombed Pearl Harbor, Hawaii. The U.S. entered **World War II** the next day. Ted joined the U.S. Army on January 7, 1943. He was assigned to the Information and Education Division at Fox Studio in Hollywood, California. Ted and Helen had bought a vacation home in La Jolla, California in 1940. So, in 1943 they moved to California.

Ted made educational films for the army. Two of the films that Ted worked on won **Academy Awards**. In March of 1944, Ted was **promoted** to major. In August of 1945, the war ended. Ted was looking forward to his **discharge** from the service.

Ted was discharged on January 13, 1946. He and Helen decided to stay in California. They bought land around an observation tower in La Jolla and built a house there. Soon, he began writing his next book.

A crew of filmmakers shoot a movie for the U.S. Army. This is the kind of work Dr. Seuss did during the war.

The Cat in the Hat

*T*ed's first book after the war was *McElligott's Pool*. He wrote *Bartholomew and the Oobleck* in 1949. These books were so popular that they were nominated for **Caldecott Medals**.

Ted wrote *The Cat in the Hat* in 1957 using only 225 easy-to-read words. Ted thought it would be easy to write a book using so few words. It wasn't. It took him a long time. But when he finished it, he wanted to write more stories that children would be able to read by themselves.

In 1958, Ted, Helen, and **editor** Phyllis Cerf founded Beginner Books. They put the image of the Cat from *The Cat in the Hat* on the cover of each new book.

Helen wrote and edited stories for the company and helped answer the mail Ted received from his fans. She often signed her letters "Mrs. Dr. Seuss."

Dr. Seuss won many awards for his movies and books.

The Grinch

*I*n 1957, Ted wrote *How the Grinch Stole Christmas.* The Grinch was his favorite of all the characters he created. He often joked that he was part Grinch himself. He chose GRINCH as the letters on his car's license plate.

The message of the book was important to Ted. He felt that too many people spend Christmastime shopping and thinking about presents. He wanted to remind them to think about love and friendship instead of gifts.

Later, Ted wrote a television version of *How the Grinch Stole Christmas.* It won a **Peabody Award**. That was followed by "Halloween is Grinch Night" and "The Grinch Grinches the Cat in the Hat." Both of these films won **Emmy Awards**.

Ted kept busy writing and illustrating new stories. Whenever Ted finished a book, he went to New York to read it aloud to the editors at Beginner Books. He wanted to hear them laugh. If Ted did not think the pages were funny enough, he would rewrite them. He worked hard to make each story as good as it could be.

After Ted proved he could write using just a few words, his **publisher**, Bennett Cerf, challenged him to write a book using only 50 words. He bet $50 that Ted could not do it. Ted accepted the bet.

In 1960, Ted wrote *Green Eggs and Ham* using exactly 50 words. Years later, Ted said the eggs he invented might not have been such a good idea. People kept trying to feed him green eggs!

Watching "How the Grinch Stole Christmas" has become a holiday tradition for many families.

New Places to Go

*T*ed loved to travel, and he loved to read. He read four or five books each week. He saw life as a changing adventure for everyone, young or old.

Ted worried about the environment. In 1971, he wrote *The Lorax* to show people how the earth, air, and water are destroyed when forests are cut down. In 1984, he wrote *The Butter Battle Book* to make people think about nuclear war.

Ted's books had helped millions of children learn to read. They also taught serious lessons in a fun way. People young and old loved his books. In 1984, Ted won the **Pulitzer Prize**.

Ted's last book was **published** in 1990. It is an inspiring book about the future. *Oh, the Places You'll Go!* reminds readers that life is a journey and "You have brains in your head, you have feet in your shoes, you can steer yourself any direction you choose."

Ted always looked ahead to the "Great Places." That is why he did not retire. Even when his eyesight began to fail, he managed to keep working.

But Ted was getting older. Soon he became sick. On September 24, 1991, Theodor Seuss Geisel, known by millions of fans as Dr. Seuss, died. But his books live on and continue to educate people with their catchy **rhymes** and unforgettable characters.

Dr. Seuss's books continue to educate and entertain children all over the world.

Dr. Seuss Lives On

*D*r. Seuss's stories have delighted readers for over 60 years. He wrote and illustrated over 50 children's books. Some have been made into movies and TV shows.

But Dr. Seuss did more than write books. He used the money he made to help others. He gave money to libraries, art museums, and zoos. He created **scholarships** to help students go to college. Many libraries celebrate his birthday with special reading programs.

Dr. Seuss has also inspired people to improve the environment. A group created The Lorax Project to bring new trees to areas which had been damaged. The Dr. Seuss Lorax Forest has been created in Francis Marion National Forest near Charleston, South Carolina.

The people of Springfield are especially proud of Dr. Seuss. They built a Dr. Seuss National Memorial in their city park. It has statues of many of his creatures to remind visitors of the wonderful world Dr. Seuss brought to life.

The Cat in the Hat and his friends star in "The Wubbulous World of Dr. Seuss," the first television series based on Seuss's characters.

Glossary

Academy Award - an award given by the Academy of Motion Picture Arts and Sciences to the best films of the year.

Caldecott Medal - an award given by the American Library Association to the author of the year's best picture book. Books that are runners-up are called Caldecott Honor Books.

concentrate - to focus all of your attention on something.

dean - the person at a university who is in charge of the students.

discharge - to be released from military service.

edit - to correct, improve, or prepare for publication. A person who does this is called an editor.

editorial cartoons - a cartoon that expresses an opinion of the editor, publisher, or owner of a newspaper or magazine.

Emmy Award - an award given by the Academy of Television Arts and Sciences to the year's best television programs and actors.

fascinate - to grab and hold someone's attention.

landlord - a person who owns houses or apartments that people rent.

Peabody Award - an award given by the University of Georgia for achievement and public service by radio and television networks.

pen name - the name an author uses that is different form his or her own.

promoted - to get a raise to a higher rank or position.

publish - to produce and offer printed materials for sale to the public. A publisher is someone who does this for a business.

Pulitzer Prize - an award established by journalist Joseph Pulitzer for achievement in journalism, literature, drama, and music.

rhythm - a regular repetition of sounds or movements.

rhyme - the repetition of the same sounds at the end of the lines of a verse.

scholarship - a gift of money to help a student pay for instruction.

World War II - 1939 to 1945, fought in Europe, Africa, and Asia. The United States, France, Great Britain, the Soviet Union, and their allies were on one side. Germany, Italy, Japan, and their allies were on the other side. The war began when Germany invaded Poland. America entered the war in 1941 after Japan bombed Pearl Harbor, Hawaii.

Internet sites

Welcome to Seussville!

www.randomhouse.com/seussvllle/

This is Dr. Seuss's official Web site at Random House. Play games, compete in trivia contests, ask the Cat a question, and much more!

Index